FLORIDA KEYS BUCKET LIST

David L. Sloan

PHANTOM **PRESS**

For use of information contained as source material, credit: David L. Sloan, author, *The Florida Keys Bucket List.*

Editorial services: DorothyDrennen.com

Inquiries: david@phantompress.com

ISBN: 978-0-9831671-8-1

HOW TO USE

1. **WHAT TO EXPECT**

   This isn't the kind of guidebook that will hold your hand every step of the way. Instead, the book lists 100 offbeat adventures in the Florida Keys and provides a little bit of local commentary to give you an idea of what you are in for. Consider each page a primer for adventure.

2. **FINDING THINGS**

   While the book provides general directions, most people will find that using Google Maps on a smart device is the way to go. Most directions in the Florida Keys involve Mile Markers. Mile Marker 0 is in Key West. Mile Marker 108 is in Key Largo. To get a sense of which Mile Marker a location is near, remove the last three digits of the mailing or street address to find the Mile Marker.

3. **WARNINGS**

   Some of the activities may be dangerous or illegal. Use common sense. Do them all at your own risk.

4. **BEST RESULTS**

   Go at your own pace. If one of the items looks stupid to you — skip it. If you are unsure about an item — Google it and do some more research. If you love an item — check it off twice. Bucket Lists are about personal growth and achievement. Stepping out of your comfort zone is a good thing. No matter how you approach the offbeat adventures in this book, you'll find one of the best aspects is the memories you make and the people you meet along the way.

ADVENTURES

FLORIDA CITY

1. DRIVE ON A CORAL REEF
2. HOLD A BABY GATOR
3. SEE IF ROBERT IS THERE
4. TOAST WARREN ZEVON
5. TAKE THE OLD ROAD
6. GET A TASTE OF ALABAMA JACK'S
7. SEARCH FOR THE SKUNK APE

KEY LARGO

8. SEARCH FOR CAESAR'S ROCK
9. GET A TASTE OF KEY LARGO
10. SLEEP WITH THE FISH
11. EXPLORE AN UNDERWATER STATE PARK
12. VISIT CHRIST OF THE DEEP
13. EXPLORE A DESERTED ISLAND
14. DIVE THE SPIEGEL GROVE
15. SEE THE WHALING WALLS
16. CRUISE ON THE AFRICAN QUEEN
17. TICKLE A CRUSTACEAN
18. SEE THE GLASS BOTTOM BAR
19. HUNT FOR SUNKEN TREASURE

ISLAMORADA

20. **DO ONE FOR THE BIRDS**
21. **SEE TOILET SEAT CUT**
22. **BUTTER UP TO BETSY THE LOBSTER**
23. **SWIM WITH PARROT FISH**
24. **PAINT WITH A SEA LION**
25. **WALK A SMUGGLER'S TRAIL**
26. **HAVE A RUMRUNNER WHERE IT WAS INVENTED**
27. **PARTY ON A SANDBAR**
28. **REEL IN A BLUE MARLIN**
29. **SAMPLE LOCAL BREWS**
30. **LEAVE A FLOWER AT THE HURRICANE MEMORIAL**
31. **CELEBRATE THE FULL MOON KEYS STYLE**
32. **CLIMB ABOARD THE PILAR**
33. **GET A TASTE OF ZANE GREY**
34. **HAND FEED A GIANT TARPON**
35. **EAT LIONFISH**
36. **KAYAK TO A GHOST TOWN**
37. **RAISE A TOAST AT THE DEAD ANIMAL BAR**
38. **FISH A GRAND SLAM**
39. **DROP A LINE OFF THE CHANNEL #5 BRIDGE**
40. **CAMP AT LONG KEY**
41. **HIKE THE GOLDEN ORB TRAIL**
42. **WATCH THE SUNSET IN YOUR REAR VIEW MIRROR**
43. **FIND YOUR OWN KOKOMO**
44. **TAKE A BLOODLINE TOUR**

MARATHON TO BAHIA HONDA

45. **EXPLORE A MANGROVE TUNNEL**
46. **WAKEBOARD IN A QUARRY**
47. **VISIT FLIPPER'S GRAVE**
48. **MUNCH ON A KEY COLONY INN FISH SANDWICH**
49. **HAND-FEED A SHARK**
50. **EXPLORE ADDERLEY'S HOUSE**
51. **WATCH A SEA TURTLE RELEASE**
52. **INDULGE IN DEEP FRIED KEY LIME PIE**
53. **FEAST ON STONE CRAB CLAWS**
54. **FLY OVER THE SEVEN-MILE BRIDGE IN A HELICOPTER**
55. **DISCOVER PIGEON KEY**
56. **SEARCH FOR BIG MO**
57. **DANGLE YOUR LEGS OFF THE BAHIA HONDA BRIDGE**
58. **SNORKEL THE BRIDGE PILINGS**
59. **DRIVE A RANDOM SIDE ROAD**
60. **CATCH SUNRISE ON THE WATER**
61. **SEND A COCONUT POSTCARD**
62. **SWIM IN THE GULF & THE OCEAN AT THE SAME TIME**

BIG PINE KEY TO STOCK ISLAND

63. **ROAM AN EXOTIC ORCHARD**
64. **SPOT A KEY DEER**
65. **LEAVE YOUR NAME AT NO NAME PUB**
66. **SIGNAL THE UFOS**
67. **SEE A BABY MANATEE**
68. **FIND A GATOR AT THE BLUE HOLE**

KEY WEST AND BEYOND

FLORIDA CITY

GATEWAY TO THE KEYS

1

DRIVE ON A CORAL REEF

WHAT'S THE DEAL?
Most people don't realize that the very islands that make up the Keys were once thriving coral reefs. Sea levels fluctuated and exposed the reefs, we built a road across them, and today, that road allows us to drive more than 100 miles into the ocean. A drive down the Overseas Highway is a trip everybody should make at least once.

DO IT IF: You want to fully experience a significant part of the Keys experience.

SKIP IT IF: You drive like a jerkoff.

LOCAL ADVICE: Take it slow. People who get impatient and try to pass don't get anywhere fast. Some of them end up dead, and that totally ruins a vacation.

I DID IT:

DID YOU KNOW?

The Overseas Highway spans 113 miles of roadway and includes 42 overseas bridges.

2

HOLD A BABY GATOR

WHAT'S THE DEAL?
Alligators are a star attraction in Florida, and no trip past the Everglades is complete without some kind of alligator encounter. Spotting them in the wild is cool, but it doesn't compare to the close encounters available at the Everglades Alligator Farm *(everglades.com)*. In addition to snake and alligator shows, they have alligator feedings and airboat rides. Snap your photo holding a baby gator and your friends on social media will know you are wild and brave.

DO IT IF: You want to hold an animal in your hands that could eat you 10 years from now.

SKIP IT IF: Your mother was killed by an alligator.

LOCAL ADVICE: The gators are more active in the morning. Try to get a seat toward the front of the airboat.

I DID IT: ☐

DID YOU KNOW?

South Florida is the only place in the world where alligators and crocodiles coexist.

3

SEE IF ROBERT IS THERE

WHAT'S THE DEAL?
The ground in the Florida Keys is terrible for farming, so we never miss a chance to grab fresh produce from Redland, Florida. A roadside stand called Robert Is Here *(robertishere.com)* has become an exotic fruit mecca offering over 500 varieties of exotic fruit through the year. Think jackfruit, guanabana, and sugar apple. The place is family owned and operated and hosts a small zoo in the back with a lot of crazy characters. It's a short jaunt off the highway. You might even meet Robert.

DO IT IF: You want an exotic fruit milkshake that you will remember for years.

SKIP IT IF: You think fruit is stupid and hate local flavor.

LOCAL ADVICE: Try a cherry-Key lime shake or one of the exotic smoothies. Boiled peanuts make a great snack for your drive.

I DID IT:

DID YOU KNOW?

Robert Moehling started his business as a child with a card table, a few cucumbers and a sign proclaiming "Robert Is Here."

4

TOAST WARREN ZEVON

WHAT'S THE DEAL?
You probably love Warren Zevon or have no idea who he is. Don't worry; he is dead and probably doesn't care either way. Warren was a musician who had hits with *Werewolves Of London* and *Lawyers, Guns and Money.* He used to visit the Keys with Carl Hiaasen and his final album, Mutineer, was inspired in part by the Mutineer Restaurant *(mutineerrestaurant.wordpress.com)* in Florida City. Grab a stool at the bar and check out the YouTube video for his song Mutineer over a cold one.

DO IT IF: You like to frequent places that inspired songs.

SKIP IT IF: You could care less about Warren Zevon or cold beer.

LOCAL ADVICE: It's usually happy hour here. Skip tables and opt for a barstool in the Wharf Lounge.

I DID IT: ☐

DID YOU KNOW?

Warren Zevon and South Florida author Carl Hiaasen co-wrote the song *Basket Case* for Zevon's 2002 album *My Ride's Here.*

5

TAKE THE OLD ROAD

WHAT'S THE DEAL?
When driving down the Keys from the mainland you have a choice of taking US1 or Card Sound Road. Both are good, but the more unusual and adventurous route is Card Sound Road. Alabama Jack's is the main draw, but the view as you drive over the bridge has bragging rights of its own. Much of the drive is through wooded skunk ape territory, and though the route is slightly longer than US1, there is usually less traffic. The route is a hot spot for shooting stars at night.

DO IT IF: You want to check-off items five, six and seven in this book.

SKIP IT IF: You are too cheap to pay the $1.00 toll.

LOCAL ADVICE: Pull over by one of the bridges and dip your toes in the water.

I DID IT: ☐

DID YOU KNOW?

Road construction on what would become Card Sound Road started on June 20, 1924.

6

GET A TASTE OF ALABAMA JACK'S

WHAT'S THE DEAL?
Alabama Jack's is a biker-tiki-dive bar and restaurant located in downtown Card Sound, which basically is the middle of nowhere. Jimmy Buffett references the place in one of his books, Bloodline filmed scenes here, and the 1994 Wesley Snipes action film Drop Zone built the main bar as part of their set. This is a traditional first stop in the Keys. Their beer is cold and the conch fritters have a reputation.

DO IT IF: You would like to try the best conch fritters in the Keys.

SKIP IT IF: Wesley Snipes movies make you cry.

LOCAL ADVICE: Sit at the bar, but be sure to check out the water's edge to see what is lurking around.

I DID IT: ☐

DID YOU KNOW?

Jack "Alabama Jack" Stratham was from Sumpter County, Georgia — not Alabama.

7

SEARCH FOR
THE SKUNK APE

WHAT'S THE DEAL?
If you think the Keys are immune from a bigfoot-like beast that is part man and part ape, you are mistaken. Skunk ape legends go back hundreds of years in Native American legend, and the creature has been sighted as far south as Key Largo. The wooded area surrounding Card Sound Road is a ripe habitat. Watch the side of the road and keep your eyes peeled.

DO IT IF: You would like to do something other than look at trees on the northern leg of Card Sound Road.

SKIP IT IF: *Finding Bigfoot* left you empty inside.

LOCAL ADVICE: Sightings still happen, but the only regular one is at The Last Chance Saloon.

I DID IT: ☐

DID YOU KNOW?

The Skunk Ape is also known as Swamp Cabbage Man, Swampsquatch, and the Florida Bigfoot.

KEY LARGO

DIVE CAPITAL OF THE WORLD

SEARCH FOR CAESAR'S ROCK

WHAT'S THE DEAL?

Legends abound about a pirate named Black Caesar who used to patrol the Keys. One story says Caesar drove a large iron ring into a rock and used it to pull his ship's mast down close to the water so as not to be seen by ships he was about to attack. Another story says he chained his prisoners to this very same rock and left them to suffer the elements. A rock with an iron ring believed to be Caesar's Rock was discovered, but its location has been lost to time. Perhaps you will rediscover it?

DO IT IF: You want a Goonies-style adventure.

SKIP IT IF: You believe that modern pirates took the ring.

LOCAL ADVICE: According to some legends, the rock was located in Key Largo. You will have to use your own treasure hunting skills on this one.

I DID IT: ☐

DID YOU KNOW?

Local historians believe the ring from Caesar's Rock was sent to the Smithsonian.

GET A TASTE OF KEY LARGO

WHAT'S THE DEAL?
Key Largo, Florida was named after Key Largo the movie. In fact, the screenplay was written at The Caribbean Club *(caribbeanclubkl.com)*. The Caribbean Club is a dive bar with an old Florida feel and million dollar views, but you will want to visit because it is a Key Largo tradition. Bloodline filmed several scenes here and Jimmy Buffett said, "It was a bar like many others and then it wasn't."

DO IT IF: You can't pass up a good old Florida dive bar on the water.

SKIP IT IF: Smokey, cash only bars don't float your boat.

LOCAL ADVICE: Mile Marker 104. Stop in around sunset for an incredible view. Check out the old Mile Marker post out back. It's one of the last remaining.

I DID IT: ☐

DID YOU KNOW?

"Key Largo" comes from the Spanish "Cayo Largo" meaning "long key."

10

SLEEP WITH THE FISH

WHAT'S THE DEAL?
Where else but Key Largo could you sleep with the fish in an underwater hotel? If you said, "nowhere," you are correct. Jules' Undersea Lodge *(jul.com)* started as a research laboratory and evolved into the coolest dive hotel around. Celebrities like Steven Tyler of Aerosmith love to stay here, but regular Joes are welcome too.

DO IT IF: You want to wake up with an angelfish giving you the eye.

SKIP IT IF: The thought of sleeping in a submerged cabin takes your breath away.

LOCAL ADVICE: 51 Shoreland Drive near Mile Marker 103. Don't miss the underwater pizza delivery. Skype your friends to show then how cool you are.

I DID IT: ☐

DID YOU KNOW?

Jules' Undersea Lodge was formerly the La Chalupa Research Laboratory in Puerto Rico.

11

EXPLORE AN UNDERWATER STATE PARK

WHAT'S THE DEAL?
The famous John Pennekamp Coral Reef State Park *(floridastateparks.org/park/pennekamp)* was the first underwater park in the United States. The coral reefs are the main attraction, and can be viewed by snorkeling, scuba diving, or glass bottom boat. The park includes about 70 nautical square miles of the Atlantic Ocean. This is one of the best introductions to the underwater world of the Keys.

DO IT IF: You want to feel like you are in the biggest aquarium in the world.

SKIP IT IF: You are looking for a sandy beach to relax on.

LOCAL ADVICE: Mile Marker 102.6. The weather makes or breaks the best activities. Check water temperatures and winds before you go.

I DID IT:

DID YOU KNOW?

John Pennekamp Coral Reef State Park was added to the National Register of Historic Places on April 14, 1972.

12

VISIT CHRIST OF THE DEEP

WHAT'S THE DEAL?
Christ of the Deep is an 8½ foot tall, 4000 pound bronze sculpture of Jesus Christ that stands in 25 feet of water off of Key Largo. Dedicated in 1966, the statue is the most popular underwater site in the Florida Keys. It can be visited by snorkel, scuba or glass bottom boat trip. *(keysdiver.com)*

DO IT IF: You want to visit the most iconic and talked about underwater location in the Florida Keys.

SKIP IT IF: Weather conditions are unfavorable.

LOCAL ADVICE: This is a hot spot, so expect crowds. Don't forget to bring an underwater camera. Snorkelers will want to go on a day with good visibility.

I DID IT: ☐

DID YOU KNOW?

> The original casting of this statue is located in the Mediterranean Sea near Genoa, Italy.

13

EXPLORE A DESERTED ISLAND

WHAT'S THE DEAL?

There are over 1700 islands in the Florida Keys. Most of them are very small, and the majority of them are not populated. This means there are more than a thousand opportunities for you to escape civilization and explore on your own. Only 43 of our islands are connected by bridges, so find a friend with a boat.

DO IT IF: You want to see how Ginger and the Professor felt.

SKIP IT IF: Nature freaks you out.

LOCAL ADVICE: Exploring by kayak takes things to a new level. Check out Florida Bay Outfitters *(paddlefloridakeys.com)* in Key Largo for kayak rentals.

I DID IT: ☐

DID YOU KNOW?

The term "key" comes from the Spanish "cayo" meaning "small island."

14

DIVE THE SPIEGEL GROVE

WHAT'S THE DEAL?
The USS Spiegel Grove was a Thomaston-class dock landing ship of the United States Navy. She became an artificial reef in 2002 when she sank prematurely during a strategic sinking that didn't go as planned. This sinking left her on her side on the sea bottom with her bow protruding. In a rare stroke of fortune, a 2005 hurricane shifted her keel right side up and into the position originally intended. She is enormous in size, and larger than most natural reefs in the Keys. This is just one of the reasons she sees more than 50,000 dives each year.

DO IT IF: You want one of the best dive experiences in the United States.

SKIP IT IF: You are not certified to dive.

LOCAL ADVICE: This is a big wreck. Check out a map so you know where you are. Fishermen love it too. Watch for hooks and lines. Skip this if you are not an advanced, certified diver. *(horizondivers.com)*

I DID IT: ☐

DID YOU KNOW?

Spiegel Grove was named after the Freemont, Ohio estate of President Rutherford B. Hayes.

15

SEE THE WHALING WALLS

WHAT'S THE DEAL?
Marine artist Wyland had the goal of creating 100 life-size marine murals to reshape attitudes about marine life conservation. Over the course of 27 years, his Whaling Wall campaign became one of the largest Art in Public Places projects in history and spanned 5 continents, 13 countries and 79 cities. Three of these murals are found in the Florida Keys. Snap a photo in front of each of them. Mile Marker 55.5, Mile Marker 99.2, 201 William Street.

DO IT IF: Really big murals turn you on.

SKIP IT IF: You think art is stupid.

LOCAL ADVICE: Wikipedia has a good list of all 100 walls. *(en.wikipedia.org/wiki/List_of_Whaling_Walls)* Number 95 is in Key Largo, number 27 in Marathon, and number 52 in Key West. For best results, check these off as you complete other bucket list items.

I DID IT:

DID YOU KNOW?

Wyland selected the paint color for the concrete barriers on the Overseas Highway's 18-mile stretch. It's called "Belize Blue."

16

CRUISE ON
THE AFRICAN QUEEN

WHAT'S THE DEAL?

The African Queen is a 1951 adventure film starring Humphrey Bogart, Katharine Hepburn, and a tramp steamer called the African Queen *(africanqueenflkeys.com)*. After the film, the tramp steamer had an interesting journey that included operating charters in Oregon and languishing in an Ocala, Florida cow pasture. Today, she has been restored to her original Hollywood splendor, and she thrills guests with daily canal and dinner cruises.

DO IT IF: You want to experience a real piece of movie history.

SKIP IT IF: Your grandmother cheated on your grandfather with Humphrey Bogart.

LOCAL ADVICE: Mile Marker 99.7. Ask the captain for a turn at the helm. Don't forget to blow the whistle.

I DID IT: ☐

DID YOU KNOW?

The African Queen was built in Lytham, England in 1912 for service in Africa for the East Africa British Railway Company.

17

TICKLE A CRUSTACEAN

WHAT'S THE DEAL?
The Florida Keys are famous for the spiny or Caribbean lobster that make their homes in the surrounding waters. Eating them is great, but nothing compares to catching your own lobster and taking it every step of the way from the water to your stomach. In addition to being a great way to spend time with family or friends, it is decent exercise in beautiful water, and you are rewarded with delicious feast. This can only be done in season, and requires a permit.

DO IT IF: You like to be rewarded for your efforts with food.

SKIP IT IF: You squirm like a sissy when you touch live animals.

LOCAL ADVICE: Check out this article to become an expert before you go: *(https://www.saltstrong.com/articles/how-to-catch-lobster-in-the-fl=keys)* Befriend a local to take you on your first trip.

I DID IT:

DID YOU KNOW?

Spiny lobsters can navigate by detecting the earth's magnetic field.

18

SEE THE GLASS BOTTOM BAR

WHAT'S THE DEAL?

Everybody wants waterfront dining, but the Pilot House in Key Largo *(pilothousemarina.com)* takes things up a notch by providing a bar with 30 reinforced glass floor panels that allow you to see the fish swimming below as you sip your favorite cocktail. Don't worry if water views and fish at your feet don't float your boat; Pilot House has 12 large flat screens and they often feature live bands. The Pilot House is a local favorite.

DO IT IF: You want good, fresh seafood in a casual environment with a view.

SKIP IT IF: You get vertigo standing a few feet above the water.

LOCAL ADVICE: 13 Seagate Blvd. off Mile Marker 99.5. Use the fish feeding tubes to attract more action. More fish come out under the lights at night.

I DID IT: ☐

DID YOU KNOW?

The Pilot House Marina has fifty-five boat slips and can accommodate boats up to 85 feet in length.

19

HUNT FOR SUNKEN TREASURE

WHAT'S THE DEAL?
Dozens of sunken Spanish galleons remain undiscovered off the coast of Florida. They hold tons of gold and silver but are obscured by shifting sands. Someone will stumble upon them someday and it might as well be you. The Florida Keys are ripe hunting grounds. Make any activity that you do on the water double as a treasure hunt. It adds a new layer of excitement and could make you rich.

DO IT IF: You would like to own a gold bar that weighs more than a baby seal.

SKIP IT IF: The though of discovering treasure always bored you as a child.

LOCAL ADVICE: Keep an eye out for the unusual. There are a lot of things waiting to be discovered on the ocean floor.

I DID IT: ☐

DID YOU KNOW?

Mel Fisher was a chicken farmer turned treasure hunter who discovered the $450 million motherlode of the Spanish galleon *Atocha*.

20

DO ONE FOR THE BIRDS

WHAT'S THE DEAL?
Birds are a big part of the Florida Keys experience, but sometimes they need a little help from humans. The Florida Keys Wild Bird Rehabilitation Center *(keepthemflying.org)* provides that help. You can see the results at their Key Largo facility. It is a great place to spend an hour with Center residents like Flop, Professor Moody, and other birds that are not able to be released back into the wild due to permanent conditions and injuries. Admission is free. Donations are appreciated.

DO IT IF: You like birds or feel good when you support an excellent cause.

SKIP IT IF: Injured birds remind you of the time you shot a robin with a slingshot and the memory reduces you to tears.

LOCAL ADVICE: Mile Marker 92. Call ahead so you can make sure to arrive during feeding time: (305) 852-4486

I DID IT:

DID YOU KNOW?

The Wild Bird Center offers the only known saltwater tidal ponds in Monroe County.

ISLAMORADA

SPORT-FISHING CAPITAL OF THE WORLD

21

SEE TOILET SEAT CUT

WHAT'S THE DEAL?
When you've got to go, you've got to go. And in the Keys you have got to go to Toilet Seat Cut. Located in the Florida Bay around Mile Marker 90 in Tavernier, about 250 toilet seats line a 60-foot wide channel that enables travel between the east and west ends of Plantation Key. It has become an unofficial tourist attraction, and the artistic display continues to grow as people commemorate weddings, birthdays and other milestones with the addition of a newly decorated toilet seat at the cut. Read the cut's history here: *(http://www.allatsea.net/how-toilet-seat-cut-in-islamorada-came-to-be/)*

DO IT IF: You want to see a funky attraction that isn't in most of the guidebooks yet.

SKIP IT IF: You don't want to go on the water because there is another toilet seat you need to stay close to.

LOCAL ADVICE: Bring your camera and get ready to pose. Even *Bloodline* left a toilet seat here.

I DID IT: ☐

DID YOU KNOW?

> The first toilet seat to arrive in Toilet Seat cut was delivered by Hurricane Donna in 1960.

22

BUTTER UP TO BETSY THE LOBSTER

WHAT'S THE DEAL?
Betsy is the world's largest spiny lobster, but she is not one you would want to eat. Created in the 1980's by artist Richard Blaze, Betsy is a landmark sculpture that greets visitors to the Rain Barrel Artisan Village *(86700 Overseas Highway)*. Measuring in at 30-feet tall and 40-feet long, Betsey is hard to miss, and you would have to be crazy to drive past her without stopping for a quick photo opportunity.

DO IT IF: You can't resist giant sculptures of animals.

SKIP IT IF: You don't want your friends on social media to see how cool you look standing beside the world's largest spiny lobster.

LOCAL ADVICE: Pose like the lobster is about to attack you for added effect.

I DID IT:

DID YOU KNOW?

A photograph of Warren Zevon posing with Betsy the Lobster appears in his 2009 biography, *I'll Sleep When I'm Dead*.

23

SWIM WITH PARROT FISH

WHAT'S THE DEAL?
Parrot fish are like rainbows in the sea – their striking colors make for great photos. You can feed them at the beach area of Theater Of The Sea *(theaterofthesea.com)* or even better, join them in the water and surround yourself with food pellets for an experience you won't forget.

DO IT IF: You want to immerse yourself in a sea of color.

SKIP IT IF: You suffer from ichthyophobia.

LOCAL ADVICE: Mile Marker 84.7. Bring quarters for the fish food machine. Don't think about the sharks in the neighboring lagoon.

I DID IT:

DID YOU KNOW?

Parrotfish are named for the tightly packed teeth on the external surface of their jawbone that form a parrot-like beak.

24

PAINT WITH A SEA LION

WHAT'S THE DEAL?
For about $100 you can spend time creating a masterpiece work of art with a resident sea lion at Theater Of The Sea *(theaterofthesea.com)*. Proceeds from the program go towards animal enrichment at the park and price includes park admission. Theater Of The Sea features dolphin, sea lion, and parrot shows as well as a bottomless boat ride and nature tour. It's a pretty cool place to spend the day, and the painting makes a one-of-a-kind souvenir.

DO IT IF: You want to spend time with someone who paints on your skill level.

SKIP IT IF: You already have an animal to paint with at home.

LOCAL ADVICE: Mile Marker 84.7. Choose light colors. Don't arrive with fish in your pockets.

I DID IT: ☐

DID YOU KNOW?

Sea lions have an average lifespan of 20 to 30 years.

25

WALK A SMUGGLER'S TRAIL

WHAT'S THE DEAL?
Smuggling played a huge role in the development of the Keys, but all of the stories in the world won't give you a sense of what is was like to be a smuggler. There is, however, a small trail behind Ocean View Sports Pub *(theocean-view.com)* that will. Captain Larry's Trail was a real smuggling trail. Take a walk on it through the mangroves and down to the bay where cargo was unloaded. You will feel like you were there.

DO IT IF: You want to feel like you are in an episode of Miami Vice.

SKIP IT IF: You would rather stay home and do drugs instead of getting out to see where they were once delivered.

LOCAL ADVICE: Mile Marker 84.5. Walk the trail at night for the best smuggleresque experience.

I DID IT: ☐

DID YOU KNOW?

Locals refer to the bales of cocaine and marijuana frequently found floating in the waters of the Florida Keys as "square grouper."

26

HAVE A RUMRUNNER WHERE IT WAS INVENTED

WHAT'S THE DEAL?
The Rum Runner is a popular drink made with rum, fruit liqueurs, fresh juices, and a splash of grenadine. It is popular across the globe, but was first created in Islamorada, Florida at the Holiday Isle Tiki Bar when old inventory had to be used up to make room for new and the owner challenged bartender "Tiki John" to create a new drink. The bar has changed quite a bit since the drink was invented in 1972, but the location at the Postcard Inn *(holidayisle.com)* is the same.

DO IT IF: You enjoy drinking rum and are the kind of person who likes to go to the source.

SKIP IT IF: You just got your three-month chip in Alcoholics Anonymous.

LOCAL ADVICE: Mile Marker 84. Drinking at the birthplace comes at a price. Consider sharing.

I DID IT:

DID YOU KNOW?

The famous Tiki first started serving drinks in 1969 under the name Hapi Hula Hut. In 1971 it became officially known as the Tiki Bar.

27

PARTY ON A SANDBAR

WHAT'S THE DEAL?

There is a sandbar located in the ocean about a half-mile from Windley Key and The Postcard Inn. Both locals and visitors have made it a Keys tradition to drop anchor at the sandbar and revel in the warm, shallow water. On weekends, this is the number one place to party and people-watch. Adults sip tropical drinks as children and dogs splash about.

DO IT IF: You want to spend a relaxing day on the water celebrating a true Keys tradition.

SKIP IT IF: Your anti-depressants make your skin sensitive to sunlight.

LOCAL ADVICE: Pack enough food and booze to share. You will need a boat to get to the famous sandbar. Check out *(familyfunboattours.com)*

I DID IT: ☐

DID YOU KNOW?

The single island known as Windley Key was created from two islands formerly known as the Umbrella Keys. Around 1906, Henry Flagler filled the space between the two islands for the Overseas Railroad.

28

REEL IN A BLUE MARLIN

WHAT'S THE DEAL?
Blue marlin fishing has been described as "hours of boredom interrupted by seconds of sheer terror." But the Blue Marlin is a hands-down boss-fish and one of the most exciting species of fish to catch. Go with a pro who knows what they are doing. Islamorada is full of them. Captain Skip Bradeen *(bluechiptoo.com)* has been doing it since 1964.

DO IT IF: You want to see how Santiago felt in Hemingway's *The Old Man and the Sea.*

SKIP IT IF: You really don't want to see how Santiago felt in Hemingway's *The Old Man and the Sea.*

LOCAL ADVICE: Listen to your captain.

I DID IT: ☐

DID YOU KNOW?

The blue marlin uses its bill to stun, injure, or kill while attacking a school of fish, then returns to eat them.

29

SAMPLE LOCAL BREWS

WHAT'S THE DEAL?
Islamorada has been described as "a drinking town with a fishing problem." What better way to get to know such a town than through its beer? The Islamorada Beer Company *(islamoradabeerco.com)* brews some of the finest including a popular Sandbar Sunday wheat ale and Channel Marker IPA. Locals and visitors mingle in their tasting room at 82229 Overseas Highway. Their brews are also served in most local watering holes.

DO IT IF: You are the kind of person who enjoys a finely crafted brew.

SKIP IT IF: You were just released from a court-ordered rehab.

LOCAL ADVICE: Order a flight and sample them all.

I DID IT:

DID YOU KNOW?

Islamorada Beer Company brews a Key lime coconut ale and a coffee caramel brown ale.

30

LEAVE A FLOWER AT THE HURRICANE MEMORIAL

WHAT'S THE DEAL?
The 1935 Labor Day Hurricane severely impacted the Florida Keys. Nearly 500 lives were lost and the communities of the Keys were devastated. A memorial was constructed that tells the story of the storm and remembers those who lost their lives. You can leave a flower to show you care.

DO IT IF: You want to honor those who lost their lives in the storm.

SKIP IT IF: The only hurricane you care about is served in a glass at Pat O'Brien's.

LOCAL ADVICE: Mile Marker 81.8. Flowers are nice. Pick some up if you can. Others leave pennies as a sign of respect.

I DID IT:

DID YOU KNOW?

The Hurricane Memorial's 18-foot obelisk correlates to the approximate storm surge attributed to the Labor Day Hurricane.

31

CELEBRATE THE FULL MOON KEYS STYLE

WHAT'S THE DEAL?
Nobody celebrates the arrival of a full moon quite like we do in the Florida Keys. At Morada Bay Beach Cafe *(moradabay.com/full-moon-party/)* nearly 1000 revelers gather each month to enjoy bonfires on the beach, Tiki torches lighting the palm trees, fire dancers, stilt walkers, reggae, salsa & Junkanoo bands, and a grand display of fireworks. Check Morada Bay's website for upcoming dates and current cover charges. It is a party you won't forget.

DO IT IF: You like enchanting, magical beach parties packed with people who love to dance and have fun.

SKIP IT IF: The moon is stupid and the game is on.

LOCAL ADVICE: Mile Marker 81.6. Try Pierre's Punch. 32 ounces of Parrot Bay Coconut Rum and tropical juices served in a mason jar with a glow stick.

I DID IT: ☐

DID YOU KNOW?

The Beach Cafe was conceived to evoke the feel of a beach cafe where Hawaiian and Californian surfers might relax after a day on the water.

32

CLIMB ABOARD THE PILAR

WHAT'S THE DEAL?
Pilar is the name of Ernest Hemingway's Wheeler Playmate Cabin Cruiser now on display at his home in Havana, Cuba. The sister ship to Hemingway's Pilar is a boat by the same name that serves as the centerpiece of World Wide Sportsman *(81576 Overseas Highway)* in Islamorada. Hemingway is said to have fished on the boat when he made the decision to get one just like it. There is no better way to get a sense of what life was like for Papa out on the sea than to explore this boat. They even let you climb on board and it takes you back in time.

DO IT IF: You want to see how Papa Hemingway lived on the sea.

SKIP IT IF: The Hemingway legend is overrated.

LOCAL ADVICE: While you are there, check out the fish tank, elevator, and old Parisian storefront.

I DID IT:

DID YOU KNOW?

The name "Pilar" was Hemingway's pet name for his second wife, Pauline.

33

GET A TASTE OF ZANE GREY

WHAT'S THE DEAL?
Zane Grey was an American author best known for his Western adventure novels such as *Riders of the Purple Sage.* An avid fisherman, Grey helped establish the Long Key Fishing Club in the Florida Keys. He also pioneered the fishing of sailfish. A quaint bar tucked in the corner on the second floor of Islamorada's Worldwide Sportsman *(81756 Overseas Highway)* pays tribute to the fishing legend with a great collection of Zane Grey memorabilia. It's a unique place to have a drink and toast the legend.

DO IT IF: You want to toast an American great in a different kind of Keys bar.

SKIP IT IF: Zane Grey beat your grandfather's fishing record.

LOCAL ADVICE: Mile Marker 81.5. Go near sunset for an amazing view. Try the Bloody Mary.

I DID IT:

DID YOU KNOW?

Before being published, Zane Grey was a dentist in New York City. He chose the New York location because he wanted to be close to publishers.

34

HAND FEED A GIANT TARPON

WHAT'S THE DEAL?
Tarpon are prized saltwater game fish, in part because of their great size. You can get up close and personal with hundreds of them at Robbie's Marina *(robbies.com)* where they sell buckets of bait for you to hand feed the monsters below the docks. Admission to the docks is $2. A bucket of bait is $3. The spectacle is priceless.

DO IT IF: You want to witness the power of the 'silver kings' first hand.

SKIP IT IF: A feeding frenzy is not your cup of tea.

LOCAL ADVICE: Mile Marker 77.5. Grab a beer from the cooler on your way in. Dangle your baitfish a few inches above the water for best results. Don't drop your camera in the water.

I DID IT:

DID YOU KNOW?

The practice of hand-feeding Tarpon at Robbie's started after an injured tarpon named Scarface was nursed back to health at the marina.

35

EAT LIONFISH

WHAT'S THE DEAL?
Lionfish are a beautiful yet invasive fish in the Florida Keys. They threaten native fish and the environment, so we pretty much don't want them around. Luckily, they taste really good. They have a flavor profile somewhere between snapper and hogfish with a slight butter flavor. You can do your part to diminish their presence by eating a few. Most restaurants still do not serve them, so they are a rare delicacy that most people have not tried.

DO IT IF: You are fortunate enough to see it on a daily special menu.

SKIP IT IF: You are a vegetarian or hate the environment.

LOCAL ADVICE: You can find restaurants that serve lionfish at *reef.org/restaurants*. Call ahead to see if they have it in stock.

I DID IT:

DID YOU KNOW?

Lionfish have no known predators and reproduce all year long. A mature female releases as many as two million eggs a year.

36

KAYAK TO A GHOST TOWN

WHAT'S THE DEAL?
In 1836, Indian Key became the first county seat for Dade County. At that time, it was the site of a lucrative business community that salvaged shipwrecks. Today this ghost town is only accessible by boat, and only foundations and grave markers remain. It is a fascinating place to explore and the journey is just as spectacular as the destination. Rent kayaks from the nearby Kayak Shack at Robbie's Marina *(kayakthefloridakeys.com)*.

DO IT IF: You're ready for an outdoor adventure with a very cool history.

SKIP IT IF: Kayaking feels more like work than fun to you.

LOCAL ADVICE: Learn the history before you go at the Florida Keys History Discovery Center. They have a model of what Indian Key was once like and a great history. Bring water, a camera and sunscreen. Don't go on a windy day.

I DID IT: ☐

DID YOU KNOW?

Indian Key was the site of an Indian raid on August 7, 1840. The buildings on the island were looted and burned.

37

RAISE A TOAST
AT THE DEAD ANIMAL BAR

WHAT'S THE DEAL?
The Safari Lounge *(73814 Overseas Highway)* is more commonly referred to as "The Dead Animal Bar" or "DAB" by locals and Keys residents who make this a traditional stop on trips up or down the island chain. Decorated with animal mounts that give it the feeling of an African Lodge on the ocean, Safari Lounge is worth at least one visit just so you can say you were there. The crowd is usually friendly locals.

DO IT IF: You want to mingle with the locals in a funky dive bar.

SKIP IT IF: You want to avoid mingling with the locals at all costs.

LOCAL ADVICE: Ask for Safari Tim. Try the ring hook game.

I DID IT: ☐

DID YOU KNOW?

The Netflix show Bloodline filmed scenes in Safari Lounge that included brothers John and Danny Rayburn doing shots and John throwing up out front.

38

FISH A GRAND SLAM

WHAT'S THE DEAL?
Islamorada is known as "the sport-fishing capital of the world," in part due to her immediate access to the Atlantic Ocean, Gulf Of Mexico, Florida Bay, and Everglades. An Islamorada Grand Slam honors the outstanding achievement of one angler catching tarpon, permit, and bonefish in a single day. They say catching a world record fish takes luck. Fishing a Grand Slam takes luck and skill.

DO IT IF: You can't pass up a good challenge.

SKIP IT IF: It's easier to give up than to try.

LOCAL ADVICE: Get a good fishing guide. We suggest Chris Jones *(mudpuppycharters.com)*.

I DID IT: ☐

DID YOU KNOW?

The International Game Fish Association issues certificates to anglers who successfully fish a Grand Slam. Tarpon and other large fish are "catch and release" in the Florida Keys.

39

DROP A LINE
OFF CHANNEL #5 BRIDGE

WHAT'S THE DEAL?

In 1976, the Florida Department of Transportation finished replacing all of the bridges built by Henry Flagler for his railroad. Many of the old bridges in Islamorada were turned into fishing piers. The deep channels below the bridges attract fish from both the Atlantic Ocean and the Florida Bay, making them popular fishing holes. Channel #5 Bridge *(Mile Marker 71)* is a local favorite.

DO IT IF: You are ready to reel in a big one.

SKIP IT IF: You can afford a charter boat.

LOCAL ADVICE: Go to Bud N' Mary's for rod rental, bait, fishing license info, and fishing tips. *(budnmarys.com — 79851 Overseas Highway)*

I DID IT: ☐

DID YOU KNOW?

Work on the Overseas Railroad started in 1905. It operated from 1912 to 1935 when part of it was destroyed by a hurricane.

40

CAMP AT LONG KEY

WHAT'S THE DEAL?
Long Key State Park is a 965-acre Florida State Park located near Mile Marker 67.5. With activities such as fishing, kayaking, swimming, hiking, and bird watching available in the park, the oceanfront campsites are very desirable. All sites are oceanfront and include water, electric, fire pit, and picnic table.

DO IT IF: You want to sleep under the stars and wake up by the ocean.

SKIP IT IF: You think camping is for the birds.

LOCAL ADVICE: Bring water shoes. The highway is close to the beach sites, so earplugs may be in order for light sleepers. *(floridastateparks.org/park/long-key)*

I DID IT: ☐

DID YOU KNOW?

Long Key State Park is near the site of the former Long Key Fish Camp. Famous guests included Herbert Hoover and Franklin Roosevelt.

41

HIKE THE GOLDEN ORB TRAIL

WHAT'S THE DEAL?
The Golden Orb Trail is a 1.2-mile loop trail located in Long Key State Park *(www.floridastateparks.org/park/long-key)*. The trail is quite easy to walk and will treat you to unusual plant life, tropical hammocks, mangrove swamps, and secluded views of the Atlantic Ocean. A famous murder scene from Bloodline was filmed here. You will love the Trail because it takes you away from the development of the Keys and back to how it used to be.

DO IT IF: Nature walks massage your soul.

SKIP IT IF: You think nature is stupid.

LOCAL ADVICE: Mile Marker 67.4. Bring bug spray and a bottle of water. Go in the morning if possible.

I DID IT: ☐

DID YOU KNOW?

The trail is named after the golden orb spiders, known for their intricate webs with yellow strands that shine like gold in the sun.

42

WATCH THE SUNSET IN YOUR REAR VIEW MIRROR

WHAT'S THE DEAL?
Watching the sun go down is a Keys tradition that is usually shared with friends. The same sunset becomes a completely different experience when you watch it in your rear view mirror driving the Overseas Highway without the crowds.

DO IT IF: You want to experience the sunset in a different way.

SKIP IT IF: You don't have a car.

LOCAL ADVICE: Pick out some cool tunes for the ride. Start 15 minutes before sunset and finish 15 minutes after. Get local sunset times here:
(http://www.keywestchamber.org/sunset-times.html)

I DID IT:

DID YOU KNOW?

The Overseas Highway is a Florida Scenic Highway and Florida's only Federally designated All-American Road.

43

FIND YOUR OWN KOKOMO

WHAT'S THE DEAL?

Kokomo became a popular destination with the release of the Beach Boys 1989 hit of the same name. The song referenced a place in the Florida Keys, and a savvy businessman at Holiday Isle jumped on the name. That Kokomo is gone, but plenty more exist. Kokomo is any place you go to get away from it all. There are hundreds of places like that waiting for you in the Florida Keys if you just go out looking for them. Finding your own makes it that much more special.

DO IT IF: You'll get there fast and then you'll take it slow.

SKIP IT IF: The dreamy look in your eye doesn't give a tropical contact high.

LOCAL ADVICE: Get out of your comfort zone and explore.

I DID IT:

DID YOU KNOW?

The song *Kokomo* came about when the Beach Boys were hired to come up with a song for the soundtrack of the Tom Cruise movie *Cocktail*.

44

TAKE A BLOODLINE TOUR

WHAT'S THE DEAL?
Bloodline is a critically acclaimed Netflix drama that was filmed primarily in Key Largo and Islamorada. Many locals served as extras on the three-season series, and seeking out the locations where famous scenes were filmed has become a favorite pastime for fans of the show visiting the Keys. *A Local's Guide To Bloodline, 50 Famous Film Locations In The Florida Keys (phantompress.com)* will lead you to all of the famous and infamous locations.

DO IT IF: You want to walk in the footsteps of the Rayburn family.

SKIP IT IF: Netflix? What is Netflix?

LOCAL ADVICE: Visit the bars where they filmed and make a pub crawl out of it.

I DID IT: ☐

DID YOU KNOW?

The author of this book was an extra in the final episode of Bloodline. His scene was cut.

MARATHON
TO
BAHIA HONDA

45

EXPLORE A
MANGROVE TUNNEL

WHAT'S THE DEAL?
The Keys are better known for bridges, but our tunnels are pretty spectacular too. A lot of this has to do with the fact that they are made out of mangroves — the small trees that grow in the saltwater along our coastlines and provide a habitat for all types of animals and sea creatures. Keys Kayak *(keyskayakllc.com)* can point you in the direction of Marathon's best mangrove tunnels. They can also take you on a really good guided tour.

DO IT IF: You want to include bridges and tunnels in your Florida Keys experience.

SKIP IT IF: You'll only go on kayaks with motors.

LOCAL ADVICE: Mile Marker 59.6. Go in the morning to beat the heat.

I DID IT:

DID YOU KNOW?

Mangroves are salt tolerant trees known as halophytes. They contain a complex salt filtration system to cope with salt water immersion.

46

WAKEBOARD IN A QUARRY

WHAT'S THE DEAL?
Wakeboarding is cool. Keys Cable, Otherside Boardsports Adventure Park *(keyscable.com),* makes it even cooler with a series of overhead motor cables that allow you to wakeboard in a five-acre lagoon quarry that was used by the Florida East Coast Railroad during the construction of Henry Flagler's Overseas Railroad. The adventure park is suitable for all skill levels and the elevated system makes it easier than being pulled behind a boat.

DO IT IF: You want to be as cool as Fonzie when he jumped the shark.

SKIP IT IF: Sitting on the dock of the bay is more your speed.

LOCAL ADVICE: Mile Marker 59.3. If you are interested in kite boarding, ask about their "cable for kite" lessons.

I DID IT: ☐

DID YOU KNOW?

After quarry operations ceased, the property spent 30 years as an aquaculture and research facility.

47

VISIT FLIPPER'S GRAVE

WHAT'S THE DEAL?
Mitzi the Dolphin was the original "Flipper," the role she played in the 1963 film. Mitzi died of a heart attack in 1972 and was buried on the property of the current day Dolphin Research Center *(dolphins.org)* in Grassy Key. This is a good place to swim with the dolphins or have a dolphin encounter. Mitzi's grave is marked by the statue of a life-sized dolphin and a small plaque.

DO IT IF: You want to pay respects to the original Flipper.

SKIP IT IF: Sharks are more your speed.

LOCAL ADVICE: Mile Marker 59. Don't forget to snap your photo with the giant dolphin out front.

I DID IT: ☐

DID YOU KNOW?

On the television series, Flipper was played by five female dolphins and one male dolphin.

48

MUNCH ON A KEY COLONY INN FISH SANDWICH

WHAT'S THE DEAL?
There's something special about sitting at the bar of the Key Colony Inn *(kcinn.com)*, sipping a cold beer, looking at the ocean and munching on a fried grouper sandwich. You won't find much talk about it in the guidebooks, but it is a Keys experience worth checking out.

DO IT IF: You want a darn good fried fish sandwich.

SKIP IT IF: You're saving your caloric intake for fried Key lime pie.

LOCAL ADVICE: Mile Marker 53.5. Go for lunch and sit at the bar.

I DID IT: ☐

DID YOU KNOW?

The Key Colony Inn has won the People's Choice Award for Marathon's Best Restaurant fifteen years in a row.

49

HAND-FEED A SHARK

WHAT'S THE DEAL?
The problem with hand-feeding a shark is that, well, you are hand-feeding a shark that could eat you. Aquarium Encounters (*floridakeysaquariumencounters.com*) has removed the fear factor while maintaining the excitement by creating a tank that brings you face to face with the predators, but keeps you separated by a layer of glass. The glass is equipped with holes that allow you to pass a fish though to your shark friend. It's a thrill you don't want to miss.

DO IT IF: You want to see what the shark looked like when Fonzie jumped him.

SKIP IT IF: The theme song from JAWS still haunts you.

LOCAL ADVICE: Mile Marker 53. Book early. This encounter fills up fast.

I DID IT: ☐

DID YOU KNOW?

Aquarium Encounters' shark species include nurse, blacktip, sandbar, blacknose, and bonnethead sharks.

50

EXPLORE ADDERLEY'S HOUSE

WHAT'S THE DEAL?
The George Adderley House is the oldest surviving house in the Keys outside of Key West. It is made from the mixture of burnt shell, ash, sand, and water known as "tabby." Adderley was a black immigrant from the Bahamas who came to the Keys in 1890 and built the home in 1905. His home is part of the Crane Point Museum & Nature Center *(fla-keys.com/marathon/crane-point).* The ability to explore a rare home like his is a unique treat.

DO IT IF: You want to go inside a really old house to soak in some history.

SKIP IT IF: Historic homes kill your buzz.

LOCAL ADVICE: Mile Marker 50.5. Keep an eye on the rocking chair. Some locals claim it is haunted by the ghost of Olivia Adderley.

I DID IT:

DID YOU KNOW?

George Adderley collected sponges and made charcoal, which he took to Key West to sell from his sailboat. Adderley is buried in the Key West Cemetery.

51

WATCH A
SEA TURTLE RELEASE

WHAT'S THE DEAL?
The Turtle Hospital *(turtlehospital.org)* in Marathon has
been rescuing, rehabilitating and releasing sick and injured
sea turtles since 1986. Located in the old Hidden Harbor
Motel, they offer guided educational experiences and the
chance to get up close and personal with the sea turtles on
a daily basis. Turtle releases are an occasional treat. Check
their website to see if one will be happening while you are
in town.

DO IT IF: You want to see a pretty cool creature get a second
chance.

SKIP IT IF: A snapping turtle bit you at camp and you think
all turtles belong in hell.

LOCAL ADVICE: Mile Marker 48.5. Watch out for Chuck
Norris.

I DID IT: ☐

DID YOU KNOW?

Sea turtle nesting season in Florida takes place from
May 15th through October 31st.

52

INDULGE IN
DEEP FRIED KEY LIME PIE

WHAT'S THE DEAL?
Key lime pie is the official dessert of Florida. It originated in the Florida Keys and no trip to the island chain is complete without trying at least one slice. Porky's Bayside *(porkysbaysidebbq.com)* has an award winning "Famous Fried Key Lime Pie" that was featured on the Travel Channel's "Top 5 Key Lime Pie Spots." They have served it for nearly 20 years with the same recipe.

DO IT IF: You are ready to take your Key lime pie to the next level.

SKIP IT IF: You are open and honest with your cardiologist.

LOCAL ADVICE: Mile Marker 47.5. Get a slice to share.

I DID IT:

DID YOU KNOW?

In 2006, the state legislature designated Key lime pie as Florida's official pie.

53

FEAST ON
STONE CRAB CLAWS

WHAT'S THE DEAL?
Florida stone crab claws are a seafood delicacy available from October 15 until May 15 each year. They are usually served chilled and have a taste that is a cross between crab and lobster. Part of their allure is that they are only available for part of the year. Keys Fisheries *(keysfisheries.com)* is the number one place to go for these claws in the Keys.

DO IT IF: You want to try a seafood delicacy in the Keys.

SKIP IT IF: Meat & potatoes is the only way you go.

LOCAL ADVICE: 3502 Gulfview Ave. Check out the Seafood Market. Get the best prices on stone crab claws upstairs during happy hour.

I DID IT: ☐

DID YOU KNOW?

Only the claws of the stone crab are harvested. The crab is released and will regenerate its claws.

54

FLY OVER THE SEVEN MILE BRIDGE IN A HELICOPTER

WHAT'S THE DEAL?
The Seven Mile Bridge is a famous bridge in the Florida Keys. There is a modern bridge and an old bridge, each of which connect Knight's Key to Little Duck Key. They are both considered engineering marvels. Most people see the bridges from vehicles, but the best way to appreciate these structures is flying above them in a helicopter. Check out Old City Helicopters in Marathon *(oldcityhelicopters.com)*

DO IT IF: You want to feel like Arnold Schwarzenegger in True Lies.

SKIP IT IF: You're afraid you'll feel like Jamie Lee Curtis in True Lies. Check out the scene here: *(youtube.com/watch?v=GP48k0hZuqk)*

LOCAL ADVICE: Mile Marker 47.1. Rides run about $155 per person. For an extra $50 you can add a side trip to the historic Sombrero Lighthouse. It is well worth the cost.

I DID IT: ☐

DID YOU KNOW?

The Seven Mile Bridge has been featured in True Lies, License to Kill and 2 Fast 2 Furious.

55

DISCOVER PIGEON KEY

WHAT'S THE DEAL?
Pigeon Key *(pigeonkey.net)* is a five-acre island that served as a home base for railroad workers building and operating the Old Seven-Mile Bridge as part of Henry Flagler's Key West Extension of the Florida East Coast Railway. The railroad's history is significant to the Keys as we know them today. At Pigeon Key, visitors can step back in time and learn the importance of the tiny island. $12 admission includes a ferry ride and historical tour.

DO IT IF: You are in the mood for a cool history on a funky island.

SKIP IT IF: You would rather be drinking. *(See #31)*

LOCAL ADVICE: Mile Marker 47. Most people don't know you can snorkel here. Bring snorkel gear and a picnic lunch.

I DID IT:

DID YOU KNOW?

Pigeon Key was originally known by the Spanish "Cayo Paloma," named for the flocks of white-crowned pigeons that roosted there.

56

SEARCH FOR BIG MO

WHAT'S THE DEAL?
Big Mo, short for Big Mother, is an infamous hammerhead shark that patrols the Bahia Honda Channel following the tarpon migration and preying on hooked fish. He measures a mammoth 18-feet in length and is respected as much as he is feared. Try your luck fishing between the Bahia Honda bridges and you may encounter Big Mo.

DO IT IF: You think you are brave enough to face an 18-foot hammerhead that has been known to attack boats.

SKIP IT IF: You have not set foot in the water since JAWS.

LOCAL ADVICE: Mile Marker 36.5. You're going to need a bigger boat. Check out SeaSquared charters to go on the hunt for Big Mo *(seasquaredcharters.com).*

I DID IT: ☐

DID YOU KNOW?

The distance of Big Mo's hammer from eye to eye is said to measure five feet.

57

DANGLE YOUR LEGS OFF THE BAHIA HONDA BRIDGE

WHAT'S THE DEAL?
The Bahia Honda Rail Bridge is a derelict railroad bridge connecting Bahia Honda Key with Spanish Harbor Key. It was constructed in 1905 and closed in 1972. Most visitors see the bridge from Bahia Honda State Park, but one of the most incredible views in the Keys comes from the Spanish Harbor side. Dangling your legs off the bridge where a section has been removed is an experience no one should miss.

DO IT IF: You want to experience crumbling beauty over pristine waters.

SKIP IT IF: Don't skip it.

LOCAL ADVICE: Mile Marker 36. Take a photo. It lasts longer.

I DID IT:

DID YOU KNOW?

The Overseas Railway used to stop on Bahia Honda, giving passengers an opportunity to picnic and swim.

58

SNORKEL THE BRIDGE PILINGS

WHAT'S THE DEAL?
Most people who snorkel in the Florida Keys go to the reef on a boat. Reef and boat are both unnecessary, as you can find a great variety of sea life around the old bridge pilings throughout the islands. The Spanish Harbor side of the old Bahia Honda Rail Bridge is an excellent choice. Just grab your snorkel gear and a dive flag and explore.

DO IT IF: You want to snorkel but don't have a boat to get to the reef.

SKIP IT IF: You are not a strong swimmer. This can be dangerous if you don't know what you are doing.

LOCAL ADVICE: Mile Marker 36. Watch out for currents. Watch out for Big Mo too.

I DID IT:

DID YOU KNOW?

At one time during the construction of the bridges and the Overseas Railroad, more than four thousand men were employed.

59

DRIVE A RANDOM SIDE ROAD

WHAT'S THE DEAL?
Part of the bucket list experience is stepping out of your comfort zone and experiencing new things. One of the best ways to get the unexpected in the Keys is to turn off on a side road where you have no idea what lies ahead. Sometimes the road will be a bust. Often times, it will lead to something funky and delightful.

DO IT IF: You like to be surprised.

SKIP IT IF: The main road has all the excitement you can handle.

LOCAL ADVICE: Act like you know where you are going.

I DID IT: ☐

DID YOU KNOW?

The Florida East Coast Railway was unable to rebuild after the 1935 hurricane, so the roadbed and remaining bridges were sold to the state for $640,000.

60

CATCH SUNRISE ON THE WATER

WHAT'S THE DEAL?
We're big fans of the sun in the Florida Keys, and though sunrise is not as popular as sunset, it is equally impressive. Head over to Sombrero Beach to watch the sun rise on the water. Each sunrise is unique, and chances are the one you see will be pretty damn impressive.

DO IT IF: You believe the early bird gets the worm.

SKIP IT IF: Sleeping off a hangover trumps sunrise.

LOCAL ADVICE: Off Mile Marker 50. Bring a towel or beach chair and a cup of coffee.

I DID IT: ☐

DID YOU KNOW?

The Sun Also Rises is a 1926 novel written by Key West author Ernest Hemingway.

61

SEND A COCONUT POSTCARD

WHAT'S THE DEAL?
Why send a regular postcard when you can mail the people you left behind a postcard written on an actual coconut? Coconuts are plentiful in the Keys. Look around and you will find one. Grab a few Sharpies to dress it up, place an address on it and head on over to the Post Office *(5171 Overseas Highway)* for postage. It's a postcard your friends won't forget.

DO IT IF: You want to surprise your friends back home.

SKIP IT IF: You don't want to be called Gilligan from now on.

LOCAL ADVICE: Leave room for postage.

I DID IT:

DID YOU KNOW?

Botanically speaking, the coconut is a drupe, not a nut.

62

SWIM IN THE GULF AND OCEAN AT THE SAME TIME

WHAT'S THE DEAL?
Anybody can swim in a single body of water, but to cover two bodies of water at once, there is no better place to go than the Florida Keys. The Gulf of Mexico is to the west and the Atlantic Ocean is to the east. Bridges separate the two bodies of water. Go swimming beneath any of the 42 bridges connecting us to the mainland and you will be swimming in the gulf and the ocean at the same time.

DO IT IF: You want to take over the world two bodies of water at a time.

SKIP IT IF: One body of water is more than you can handle.

LOCAL ADVICE: Either side of the Bahia Honda Rail Bridge will do the trick.

I DID IT: ☐

DID YOU KNOW?

The place where two bodies of water come together is known as a *confluence*.

BIG PINE KEY TO STOCK ISLAND

63

ROAM AN EXOTIC ORCHARD

WHAT'S THE DEAL?
Adolf Grimal was an eccentric recluse who imported fine soils and exotic fruit trees to the Florida Keys to create one of the most precious and legendary gardens in the United States. After his death, the grove suffered severe neglect, but in recent years, it has been brought back to life by the Growing Hope Initiative *(growinghopeinitiative.org)*. Grimal Grove is open on Saturdays or by appointment.

DO IT IF: You want to check out a funky, exotic orchard and support a good cause.

SKIP IT IF: Fruit groves are for hippies.

LOCAL ADVICE: Mile Marker 31. Call ahead to be sure the grove is open: (305) 923-6663.

I DID IT:

DID YOU KNOW?

Adolf Grimal was a machinist and inventor. He moved to the Keys in the 1950s to experiment with underwater 3-D photography.

64

SPOT A KEY DEER

WHAT'S THE DEAL?
The Key Deer is a sub-species of white-tailed deer that lives only in the Florida Keys. It as an endangered deer and is typically much smaller than a regular white tailed deer. Key Deer can be spotted between Bahia Honda and Sugarloaf Key, but your best chance for spotting one is on Big Pine Key, home of the National Key Deer Refuge (fws.gov/refuge/National_Key_Deer_Refuge). Less than 800 of the animals exist. Keep your eyes peeled and drive slow.

DO IT IF: You want to see a rare creature in the wild.

SKIP IT IF: You liked it when Bambi's mother was killed.

LOCAL ADVICE: 28950 Watson Blvd. Resist the urge to feed the deer. It makes them comfortable around humans and draws them to the road where they are likely to be hit.

I DID IT: ☐

DID YOU KNOW?

Male Key deer shed their antlers. When new antlers are growing they have a white velvet coating.

65

LEAVE YOUR NAME AT NO NAME PUB

WHAT'S THE DEAL?
No Name Pub is the oldest bar in the Big Pine Key area. They say it is "a nice place if you can find it," and most people find it is worth the search. Originally a general store and bait shop, the building took a turn as a brothel before becoming famous for damn good pizza and a funky decor. The walls are covered with thousands of dollar bills bearing people's names. Write your name on one and staple it up. You will be a part of No Name Key history.

DO IT IF: You like pizza and want to leave your mark in a favorite watering hole.

SKIP IT IF: You like your dollars in your pocket instead of on the wall.

LOCAL ADVICE: 30813 Watson Blvd. off Mile Marker 30.5. Bring a colorful Sharpie so your dollar stands out from the crowd.

I DID IT: ☐

DID YOU KNOW?

> In the 1960s, two cooks from Italy came to work at No Name Pub and brought a pizza recipe with them. They wrote the recipe on the kitchen wall when they left. The same recipe is still used today.

66

SIGNAL THE UFOS

WHAT'S THE DEAL?
No one is sure if they are aliens, but there are an awful lot of unidentified objects flying through the air in the Florida Keys. Some suspect the objects are military in nature. Others believe they are something from another planet. There are nearly 100 reported sightings of UFOs in the Keys on *ufo-hunters.com*. Big Pine is a hot spot, and a good place to watch the sky even if the UFOs are not around. They say you can signal them with a powerful flashlight. Who are we to argue?

DO IT IF: You want a close encounter.

SKIP IT IF: You don't want to risk an anal probe.

LOCAL ADVICE: Get away from the lights. Bring a tinfoil hat.

I DID IT: ☐

DID YOU KNOW?

The Southern Cross Astronomical Society gathers to watch the sky in Big Pine each year at the annual Winter Star Party.

67

SEE A BABY MANATEE

WHAT'S THE DEAL?
Manatees are large, gray aquatic marine mammals that live in shallow, slow moving coastal water ecosystems in the Florida Keys. Some people call them "sea cows." Keep an eye out for manatees whenever you are near a canal, marina, or shallow area of water. You'll find them in Big Pine and all of the other Keys as well. Spot a baby and it is one of the cutest things you will ever see.

DO IT IF: Baby animal videos on Facebook warm your heart.

SKIP IT IF: Baby animal videos on Facebook make you punch your computer.

LOCAL ADVICE: It's illegal, but locals like to feed the manatees lettuce and fresh water from a hose.

I DID IT:

DID YOU KNOW?

Manatees spend 50 percent of the day sleeping beneath the water. They come up for air approximately every twenty minutes.

68

FIND A GATOR
AT THE BLUE HOLE

WHAT'S THE DEAL?
The Blue Hole is an abandoned rock quarry that has filled with fresh water. Once used to mine fill for the Overseas Railroad, today it is the only fresh water lake in the Florida Keys. This makes it a favorite stop for all kinds of wildlife including Key Deer, tropical birds, iguanas, and alligators. Some refer to the local pair of gators that live at the Blue Hole as Ozzy and Sharon. No swimming in this hole.

DO IT IF: You want to kill half an hour in nature.

SKIP IT IF: You want to kill yourself in nature.

LOCAL ADVICE: Off Mile Marker 30. There are usually more animals in the morning.

I DID IT:

DID YOU KNOW?

There are over one million alligators in Florida. The name comes from the Spanish "el lagarto" meaning "the lizard."

69

CATCH A SEAPLANE
TO LITTLE PALM ISLAND

WHAT'S THE DEAL?
Little Palm Island *(littlepalmisland.com)* is a luxury resort and spa located on a private island near Mile Marker 28.5 in Little Torch Key. The resort is famous for Sunday brunch, a favorite of locals who cannot afford the price of a room at Little Palm Island but still want to experience the luxury. Whether you go for brunch or an overnight, there is no better way to arrive than in a real Key West Seaplane *(keywestseaplanes.com)*.

DO IT IF: You want to feel like a guest on Fantasy Island.

SKIP IT IF: Small planes make you scream like a little girl.

LOCAL ADVICE: Mile Marker 28.5. Watch for dolphins on the ride. See if they can swing you by any shipwrecks.

I DID IT: ☐

DID YOU KNOW?

Little Palm Island is only accessible by boat or by plane. It is a best-kept secret of United States Presidents and celebrities.

70

ATTEND THE UNDERWATER MUSIC FESTIVAL

WHAT'S THE DEAL?
Divers and snorkelers can explore the only living coral barrier reef in the continental United States while getting down and rocking out to a below the sea concert at the Lower Keys Underwater Music Festival. Taking place in July, the festival pipes music into the ocean through special speakers. The event draws several hundred participants and encourages coral reef protection.

DO IT IF: You've never attended a festival beneath the ocean.

SKIP IT IF: Coral reefs and music are overrated.

LOCAL ADVICE: Mile Marker 27.5. Wear a costume. You could win an award.

I DID IT: ☐

DID YOU KNOW?

Sound travels at about 5000 feet per second in the water compared to about 1000 feet per second in the air.

71

SAY "HEY, HEY, HEY" TO FAT ALBERT

WHAT'S THE DEAL?
Fat Albert is a tethered blimp that has been a fixture in the air over Cudjoe Key for more than 30 years. At one time Fat Albert broadcast Radio Marti to Cuba. The blimp is also used by the Air Force and NORAD in counter-drug operations. Watching the blimp as it is raised up or lowered down is pretty cool, but you can also simply admire it from afar as you chill in the water at the end of Blimp Road.

DO IT IF: You think blimps are cool.

SKIP IT IF: You are smuggling drugs.

LOCAL ADVICE: Off Mile Marker 21. Bring some water shoes and get in the water at the end of Blimp Road *(Near Mile Marker 21).* It's a secret spot that is not on most people's radar.

I DID IT: ☐

DID YOU KNOW?

Fat Albert broke loose from its tether during a storm in 1984. It drifted towards Cuba before being shot down by a Navy jet.

72

WATCH FIGHTER PLANES TOUCH & GO

WHAT'S THE DEAL?
Naval Air Station Key West is a state-of-the-art training facility for air-to-air combat fighter aircraft. Key West offers favorable flying conditions year round, and aerial ranges allow for training within minutes of takeoff. Watching the planes on their training missions is spectacular. You can often see them from the Overseas Highway as you are driving in or out of the Keys, or you can pull over on a side road if you want to watch for a while.

DO IT IF: You want to see our military in action.

SKIP IT IF: Air shows make you puke.

LOCAL ADVICE: Take Boca Chica Road *(Mile Marker 10)* to the end. Boca Chica Beach backs up to the runway.

I DID IT: ☐

DID YOU KNOW?

The U. S. Navy's presence in Key West dates back to 1823 when a Naval Base was established to stop piracy in the area.

73

DISCOVER THE
STONE SANCTUARY

WHAT'S THE DEAL?
Boca Chica Beach attracts an eclectic group of people ranging from nudists to bird watchers. A fort made of driftwood, trees, dirt, and collected garbage is built into the beach along the ocean, and is known as the Stone Sanctuary. It is said to have been built by a homeless man named Red. Much about it remains a mystery, but it is a good excuse to get yourself down to Boca Chica Beach.

DO IT IF: You want to explore a strange fort.

SKIP IT IF: The possibility of bumping into a naked person freaks you out.

LOCAL ADVICE: Bring water. It's a bit of a walk, but a beautiful one, and worth it. From Overseas Highway, head east on Boca Chica Road *(Near Mile Marker 10)*. Follow it to the end and park. The beach is straight ahead.

I DID IT:

DID YOU KNOW?

"Boca Chica" is a Spanish word meaning "small mouth."

74

FIND A CUBAN CHUG

WHAT'S THE DEAL?
"Chug" is the term for a homemade boat used by Cuban refugees to escape their homeland. The Florida Keys are about 90 miles from Cuba, so it is common for these chugs to be abandoned on our islands. Many of them become decorative fixtures in residents' yards. Others are placed in local museums. Seeing a chug in person illustrates the struggle of some Cuban people and the lengths they have been willing to go to find a better life.

DO IT IF: You want to witness Cuban ingenuity first hand.

SKIP IT IF: Castro imprisoned your relatives.

LOCAL ADVICE: Any beach is fair game, but if you want a guaranteed look at a chug, head to the Key West Botanical Garden *(kwbgs.org)*. They have several.

I DID IT: ☐

DID YOU KNOW?

In 2003, several Cubans attempted to cross the Florida Straits in a converted 1951 Chevy pick-up truck. The drive shaft was attached to a propeller and 55-gallon drums were used for floatation.

75

JUMP OFF THE SUGARLOAF BRIDGE

WHAT'S THE DEAL?
The Sugarloaf Jumping Bridge is a bridge that was part of the original Overseas Highway. It extends over a waterway known as Government Cut and serves as a place where locals gather to jump off the bridge and swim in the water below. To find the bridge, take US1 north from Key West. Turn right at Mile Marker 17 onto Sugarloaf Blvd. Follow the road until it takes a hard right. To your left you will see a yellow barrier. Park and walk past the yellow barrier to the bridge.

DO IT IF: Your friends jumped off a bridge so you would do it too.

SKIP IT IF: You are afraid of heights.

LOCAL ADVICE: Off Mile Marker 17. Bring water shoes and a six-pack of beer.

I DID IT: ☐

DID YOU KNOW?

At least one vehicle is submerged near the Sugarloaf Bridge, and is home to a massive goliath grouper.

76

PLAY JAMES BOND

WHAT'S THE DEAL?
The James Bond movie *License To Kill* was filmed in the Florida Keys. In the movie, James Bond jumps out of a plane, fights off the bad guys and parachutes down to a wedding he is attending. You don't have to fight bad guys or go to a wedding, but skydiving over the Florida Keys will take your breath away. *(skydivekeywest.com)*

DO IT IF: You want to feel like agent 007.

SKIP IT IF: You see no reason to jump out of a perfectly good plane.

LOCAL ADVICE: Off Mile Marker 17. Jump before your friends. Get the video. You'll be glad you did.

I DID IT:

DID YOU KNOW?

Because of budgetary reasons, *License To Kill* was the first James Bond film to be shot entirely outside the United Kingdom.

77

PLAY BATMAN

WHAT'S THE DEAL?
The Sugarloaf Key Bat Tower is a historic site built in 1929 by Richter Clyde Perky in an effort to combat the mosquito problem in the Lower Keys. When Perky stocked the tower with bats, they all promptly flew away and never returned. With the bats went Perky's development plans. Only three such towers exist in the United States. This one is worth checking out.

DO IT IF: You want to see a real bat tower.

SKIP IT IF: Spiderman is more your cup of tea.

LOCAL ADVICE: The Sugarloaf Key Bat Tower is about a mile off of the Overseas Highway at Mile Marker 17. Turn at the sky dive sign and keep to your right.

I DID IT:

DID YOU KNOW?

Perky attempted to attract bats to the bat tower with a secret bat bait that was said to include bat guano and the ground up sex organs of female bats.

78

VISIT A CELEBRITY SLOTH

WHAT'S THE DEAL?
We have a zoo in the Florida Keys. Believe it or not, the zoo is located at the prison and operated by the local Sheriff's department. The Monroe County Sheriff's Animal Farm *(keysso.net/miscellaneous/animal_park.htm)* was started in 1994 as a haven for homeless animals. It has blossomed into a community gem with several animals that have stolen our hearts. The stand out favorite is Mo the Sloth. He is famous in Key West.

DO IT IF: You love animals.

SKIP IT IF: A visit to jail hits too close to home.

LOCAL ADVICE: Off Mile Marker 4. The Animal Farm is located on Stock Island and is open on the second and fourth Sunday of each month from 1pm to 3pm. Tell Farmer Jeanne that David says "hello."

I DID IT:

DID YOU KNOW?

The Monroe County Sheriff's Animal Farm was started in a secured area below the elevated prison that was used for the evacuation of inmates in case of a fire.

KEY WEST

AND

BEYOND

79

VISIT ROBERT THE DOLL

WHAT'S THE DEAL?
Robert the Doll is an antique doll that is on display in the Fort East Martello Museum in Key West. He regularly tops lists of the most haunted dolls in the world, and people who visit him report all types of mishaps ranging from problems taking photographs of the doll to seeing the doll moving on his own. Robert has been featured on many paranormal television shows and is respected and feared by many.

DO IT IF: You want to see a haunted doll in person.

SKIP IT IF: Hell no.

LOCAL ADVICE: 3501 S. Roosevelt Blvd. The Internet is full of misinformation about the doll. For the real story, pick up the book *Robert the Doll* by David L. Sloan.

I DID IT:

DID YOU KNOW?

Robert the Doll was made by the Steiff Company in Germany around 1904. He was originally dressed as a clown.

INDULGE IN PINK GOLD

WHAT'S THE DEAL?
Shrimp were first harvested commercially in Key West in 1949. They were referred to as "pink gold" because of their value to the economy. Today, Key West Pinks are a staple on most menus across the island. It doesn't matter how you have them prepared. No trip to the Keys is complete without indulging in pink gold.

DO IT IF: You love seafood.

SKIP IT IF: You are allergic to shrimp.

LOCAL ADVICE: Pinks are good, but for a real treat, go to the Conch Republic Seafood Company and see if they have any Royal Reds.

I DID IT: ☐

DID YOU KNOW?

Key West shrimp don't care for the sunlight and only come out at night. The accidental discovery of this habit led to the pink gold rush.

FIND THE BEST CON LECHE

WHAT'S THE DEAL?
Café Con Leche is a popular beverage in the Florida Keys consisting of equal parts bold Cuban coffee and scalded milk. Every local has a favorite place to go for one. Try several and decide for yourself which is best. Some local favorites: Baby's Coffee, Coffee Plantation, Cuban Coffee Queen, Five Brothers, and Sandy's.

DO IT IF: You want to see what the buzz is all about.

SKIP IT IF: A nap is in your future.

LOCAL ADVICE: Café Con Leche goes really well with a Cuban cheese bread.

I DID IT:

DID YOU KNOW?

One secret to a good con leche is finely ground, dark roasted coffee beans. Cubans favor the brands Bustelo and Pilon.

82

BLOW A CONCH

WHAT'S THE DEAL?
Conch *(rhymes with "honk")* refers to natives of Key West or to the sea-dwelling mollusk that has become a symbol of our island pride. Learning to blow a conch shell has become an island right of passage. We blow conchs to start the new day or to usher the sun down. We even have an annual conch blowing competition. Blowing a conch is a true way to show your island spirit.

DO IT IF: You are feeling horny.

SKIP IT IF: You have not blown anything in years and don't plan on starting now.

LOCAL ADVICE: Make a buzzing sound while keeping your lips tightly together in the mouthpiece. You can pick up a conch shell horn at Key West Shells & Gifts *(626 Duval Street)*.

I DID IT: ☐

DID YOU KNOW?

The practice of calling natives "conchs" may have originated with the practice of people placing a conch shell on a stick in their yard to announce the birth of a child.

83

CATCH A GREEN FLASH

WHAT'S THE DEAL?
The green flash is an optical phenomenon that sometimes occurs just as the sun is setting. A green spot is visible for a split second just above the upper rim of the disk of the sun. Spotting a green flash is rare and considered a special treat or even good luck. They are more commonly seen when the sun is setting over a body of water.

DO IT IF: You want a chance to amp up your sunset experience.

SKIP IT IF: Sunsets are shady.

LOCAL ADVICE: During winter months, the best green flashes are observed from the White Street Pier.

I DID IT: ☐

DID YOU KNOW?

It is said that once you see a green flash, you will never again go wrong in matters of the heart.

84

COOL DOWN
WITH COCO FRIO

WHAT'S THE DEAL?
Chill a green coconut, slice off the top with a machete, stick in a straw and you have yourself a real Coco Frio. Coco Frio is a refreshing tropical treat on a hot summer day, but many people also drink it because it is known as "liquid Viagra." You can find it in Key West near the Hemingway Home or in the Clinton Square Market.

DO IT IF: You want a refreshing coconut drink that may put you in the mood.

SKIP IT IF: You were injured by a falling coconut as a child.

LOCAL ADVICE: Bring a small flask of rum with you to spice up the Coco Frio.

I DID IT: ☐

DID YOU KNOW?

One of the earliest mentions of coconuts dates back to the *One Thousand and One Nights* story of Sinbad the Sailor.

85

TOUR THE CEMETERY

WHAT'S THE DEAL?
The Key West Cemetery was established in 1847. It is unique in that most of the graves are above ground and it is known for the many humorous epitaphs that grace the headstones such as "I Told You I Was Sick." Open from 7AM to sunset, it is a quiet and fascinating place to spend an hour exploring.

DO IT IF: You want to explore a unique cemetery.

SKIP IT IF: You wouldn't be caught dead in a cemetery.

LOCAL ADVICE: 701 Pauline Street. Go in the morning. Grab a map from the sexton's office at the corner of Angela and Margaret Streets. The map will show you the more interesting graves.

I DID IT: ☐

DID YOU KNOW?

In 1846, a hurricane washed away most of the occupants of an earlier burial ground located near the Southernmost Point. After the hurricane a new burial ground was chosen with a higher elevation.

PREVENT A HURRICANE

WHAT'S THE DEAL?
Sister Louise Gabriel survived three major hurricanes in Key West before building Our Lady of Lourdes Grotto *(stmarykeywest.com/grotto)* on the St. Mary's Catholic Church property in 1922. She remarked that as long as the grotto stood, Key West would never experience the full brunt of a hurricane. The grotto has protected us ever since. People visit it year round to pray and light candles for continued safety.

DO IT IF: You want to visit the site of miracles.

SKIP IT IF: You want to be blown away.

LOCAL ADVICE: 1010 Windsor Lane. Go at night. The grotto is at the back of the property to the right of the church.

I DID IT:

DID YOU KNOW?

Adjacent to the grotto is the cemetery for the Sisters of the Holy Names of Jesus and Mary who died in the service of the Parish.

87

BE THE FIRST ONE AT THE SOUTHERNMOST POINT

WHAT'S THE DEAL?

The Southernmost Point Buoy is a concrete buoy at the corner of South Street and Whitehead Street; the buoy marks the southernmost point in the continental United States. It is a popular tourist attraction and one of the most photographed locations in the Florida Keys. Unfortunately this means it is crowded. Find a time to see the buoy without a crowd. This can be late night or early morning. It's an awesome location and worth the visit.

DO IT IF: You like being first.

SKIP IT IF: First is worst and last is best.

LOCAL ADVICE: Sneak a drink and celebrate your southernmostness.

I DID IT:

DID YOU KNOW?

The original monument was built at a cost of $902.17. The buoy marker weighs 19.8 tons.

88

FLOCK OFF
WITH RHETT & SCARLETT

WHAT'S THE DEAL?
The Key West Butterfly & Nature Conservatory *(keywestbutterfly.com)* is the number one attraction in Key West on TripAdvisor in part because of the amazing butterfly experience, but Rhett & Scarlett also have a little bit to do with it. Rhett & Scarlett are the conservatory's famous pink flamingos. Don't leave Key West without seeing them.

DO IT IF: You want to enter a tropical oasis.

SKIP IT IF: You are afraid of butterflies.

LOCAL ADVICE: 13116 Duval Street. Take your time. This is a great place to unwind.

I DID IT: ☐

DID YOU KNOW?

The pink, orange, or red color of a flamingo's feathers is caused by carotenoid pigments in their food.

89

CLIMB THE LIGHTHOUSE

WHAT'S THE DEAL?
A visit to the Key West Lighthouse & Keeper's Quarters *(kwahs.org/museums/lighthouse-keepers-quarters)* is a great mix of history and exploration. Eighty-eight steps lead to the top of the lighthouse and each one is exciting. Your work is rewarded with amazing views of Key West from a structure with a great history.

DO IT IF: You want a great view with a little history mixed in.

SKIP IT IF: You would rather wait until they install an elevator.

LOCAL ADVICE: They say that the tower is haunted: watch out for ghosts on your climb! The lighthouse is located at 938 Whitehead Street across from the Hemingway Home. Open daily from 9:30AM to 4:30PM.

I DID IT: ☐

DID YOU KNOW?

The first Key West lighthouse was destroyed in the Great Havana Hurricane of 1846. Fourteen people who sought refuge in the lighthouse died.

90

PLAY BINGO
WITH A DRAG QUEEN

WHAT'S THE DEAL?
Each Sunday at 5PM one of the most outrageous games of bingo you have ever seen goes down at the 801 Cabaret *(801girls.com/drag_bingo.html)*. Hosted weekly by Qmitch, this is not your mother's bingo. Filled with strong language and sexual innuendo, it is not for the faint of heart. Drag Queen Bingo has been a Sunday tradition for decades, and each week benefits a different worthy local cause.

DO IT IF: You never want to think of numbers the same way again.

SKIP IT IF: You are unable to handle a man dressed as a woman.

LOCAL ADVICE: 801 Duval Street. Sit near the front. Get more than one card. Participate as much as you can.

I DID IT: ☐

DID YOU KNOW?

Bingo evolved from a carnival game called "Beano" which was played with dried beans.

91

RELAX ON THE TREE OF SOULS

WHAT'S THE DEAL?
There is an amazing tree growing in front of the Key West Courthouse known as the "kapok tree" or the "tree of souls." According to Mayan myths, the kapok tree is sacred. The Mayans believed that the souls of the dead would climb up the branches, which reached to heaven. This is one of the most photographed trees in Key West. Sitting for a spell on her majestic roots is a grounding experience.

DO IT IF: You like being grounded.

SKIP IT IF: You think we are barking up the wrong tree.

LOCAL ADVICE: The tree of souls is located near 500 Whitehead Street. Go at night. It's a better experience.

I DID IT: ☐

DID YOU KNOW?

The Maya believe that the kapok tree is the tree of life, with roots that connect to the underworld and branches that reach the heavens. The Mayan word for "kapok" means "raised up sky."

92

STRIKE A POSE AT MILE MARKER ZERO

WHAT'S THE DEAL?
US1 runs 2,369 miles, starting in Fort Kent, Maine and ending in Key West. Florida. Snapping a photo in front of the mile zero signpost has become a popular way for people to let their friends know that they have made it to the end of the road.

DO IT IF: You want a popular Key West photo at the end of a major road.

SKIP IT IF: You don't have a camera.

LOCAL ADVICE: The sign is on Whitehead Street at the intersection with Fleming Street. While you are in the neighborhood, be sure to stop by the Green Parrot Bar for a Root Beer Barrel shot.

I DID IT:

DID YOU KNOW?

US1 is the longest north-south road in the United States.

93

HUNT GHOSTS IN OLD TOWN

WHAT'S THE DEAL?
Key West is one of the most haunted cities in the United States. Many people believe this is due, in part, to the Native American massacre that took place here. Even the name "Key West" is derived from the Spanish "Cayo Hueso" or "Island of Bones." The name was used to describe the bones strewn across the island after the massacre. Haunted Key West *(hauntedkeywest.com)* offers nightly Ghost Hunts through Old Town. It's a great way to discover the history and mysteries of the island.

DO IT IF: You ain't afraid of no ghost.

SKIP IT IF: You don't have a ghost of a chance.

LOCAL ADVICE: Book online for the best prices.

I DID IT: ☐

DID YOU KNOW?

St Paul's Church is built on top of an old burial ground. John Fleming, one of the island's original owners, is buried beneath the church altar.

94

CLIMB A MILLIONAIRE'S WIDOW'S WALK

WHAT'S THE DEAL?
William Curry was Florida's first millionaire. Today his home is known as Amsterdam's Curry Mansion Inn *(currymansion.com).* The mansion, built in 1869, is open for self-guided tours which include the rare opportunity to climb to the widow's walk at the top of the house and take in spectacular views of the city.

DO IT IF: You want a million dollar view.

SKIP IT IF: You can't climb stairs.

LOCAL ADVICE: 511 Caroline Street. Don't wear a skirt.

I DID IT: ☐

DID YOU KNOW?

The Curry Mansion Inn is also known as the birthplace of Key Lime Pie. An early version of the pie was created in the Curry Mansion Inn kitchen by Aunt Sally.

95

DRINK RUM FROM A STILL

WHAT'S THE DEAL?
Key West has a great history of people running illegal rum during prohibition, but we are fortunate enough to live in a time when real rum is made legally right here in the Florida Keys. Key West's First Legal Rum Distillery *(keywestlegalrum.com)* gives› you an opportunity to drink rum from their still.

DO IT IF: You want to taste locally made rum.

SKIP IT IF: The last time you drank rum you ended up naked in the neighbor's bushes.

LOCAL ADVICE: 105 Simonton Street. Key West's First Legal Rum distillery also makes tequila. Be sure to try it.

I DID IT: ☐

DID YOU KNOW?

During Prohibition, railroad workers would send advance notice when Federal Agents were on the train so everybody in Key West had plenty of time to hide their booze.

96

DANCE AT SLOPPY JOE'S

WHAT'S THE DEAL?
The most iconic bar in Key West has got to be Sloppy Joe's *(sloppyjoes.com)* on the corner of Duval Street and Greene Street. Ernest Hemingway drank here, and the bar has hosted a parade of interesting characters since they first opened their doors in 1933. They are open every day from 9AM to 4AM. Live music is their specialty and there is an unwritten rule that you can't go home until you hit the dance floor at Sloppy Joe's.

DO IT IF: Feet don't fail me now.

SKIP IT IF: You are suffering the agony of de feet.

LOCAL ADVICE: 201 Duval Street. The dance floor gets more crowded after sunset. This is the time to go.

I DID IT:

DID YOU KNOW?

Sloppy Joe's was originally located on Greene Street where Captain Tony's is today. Joe moved after his landlord raised the rent by one dollar.

97

CATCH SUNSET
AT MALLORY SQUARE

WHAT'S THE DEAL?
The best party in Key West takes place every night down at Mallory Square *(mallorysquare.com/sunset-celebration)* as hundreds of tourists and locals gather to watch the great ball of fire in the sky drop below the horizon over the Gulf of Mexico. Magicians, jugglers, psychics, artists, and entertainers round out the party. Grab a drink and head on down.

DO IT IF: You want to take part in a Key West tradition.

SKIP IT IF: You are a vampire.

LOCAL ADVICE: 400 Wall Street. Arrive early. The entertainment starts two hours before the sun goes down.

I DID IT: ☐

DID YOU KNOW?

The sunset celebration at Mallory Square started when groups of hippies would gather and take acid to watch the sun go down.

98

VISIT THE DRY TORTUGAS

WHAT'S THE DEAL?
No bucket list would be complete without a trip to the Dry Tortugas *(drytortugas.com).* The islands lie 70 miles off the coast of Key West and boast a massive Civil War fort in the middle of some of the most pristine waters you will find in the Keys. It is a highly desirable day trip, and one you don't want to miss.

DO IT IF: You want to explore a real piece of paradise.

SKIP IT IF: You are only in Key West for a day.

LOCAL ADVICE: Consider camping. The view of the stars at night is unparalleled.

I DID IT:

DID YOU KNOW?

The Dry Tortugas were named for the abundance of turtles in the area. "Dry" referred to the fact that no fresh water was available.

99

HOP A FLIGHT TO HAVANA

WHAT'S THE DEAL?
Did you know you can now travel legally to Cuba? You can even take a flight directly from Key West. Key West is closer to Cuba than Miami, and a visit to our neighbor is not to be missed. Hook it up with Havana Air *(havanaair.com)*.

DO IT IF: You want to visit Cuba.

SKIP IT IF: Speaking Spanish makes your tongue hurt.

LOCAL ADVICE: Consider booking a Cuban Photo Safari with Key West photographer, Rob O'Neal. He is an expert and can show you a really good time in Cuba. Email him: keywestphotos@gmail.com.

I DID IT: ☐

DID YOU KNOW?

Key West was once the cigar capital of the world. The fine tobacco was imported from Cuba and rolled in local factories.

100

CANCEL YOUR FLIGHT HOME

WHAT'S THE DEAL?
You probably have the dream of quitting your job and moving to Key West. You are not the first. A lot of people arrived here on vacation and simply never went home. Go ahead, cancel your flight and see what happens. It could be the start of a new bucket list of adventures.

DO IT IF: You are sick of the rat race and want to change your life around.

SKIP IT IF: You left the kids with a babysitter.

LOCAL ADVICE: Pick up a copy of *Quit Your Job & Move To Key West* by David L. Sloan and Chris Shultz to see if doing it is right for you.

I DID IT:

DID YOU KNOW?

Today is a perfect day to start living your dreams.

ALSO BY DAVID L. SLOAN

ABOUT THE AUTHOR

David L. Sloan quit his corporate job and moved to Key West in 1996. Since then he has authored 20 books and runs ghost tours and ghost hunts through his company Haunted Key West *(hauntedkeywest.com)*. Sloan is co-founder and co-producer of the annual Key Lime Festival *(keylimefestival.com)* and the wacky Cow Key Bridge Run Zero K *(cowkeybridgerun.com)*. He currently resides in Islamorada, Florida.

Contact: david@phantompress.com

Made in the USA
Monee, IL
07 November 2020

46965159R00066